who?

Marie Curie

마리 퀴리

Biography Comic
who? ㉒ Marie Curie

초판 1쇄 인쇄 2011년 4월 8일
초판 8쇄 발행 2013년 4월 10일

지은이 이숙자
그린이 스튜디오 청비
번역 자넷 재완 신
감수 김수희
펴낸이 김선식

4th Creative Story Team 김선영, 이유미, 김선민, 전해인, 최수아
Creative Design Dept. 박효영
Creative Management Team 김성자, 송현주, 권송이, 김민아, 윤이경, 한선미
Creative Marketing Dept. 최창규, 이주화, 이상혁, 박현미, 백미숙
          Communication Team 서선행
          Contents Rights Team 김미영

출판등록 2005년 12월 23일 제313-2005-00277호
주소 경기도 파주시 교하읍 문발리 529-2 3층, 4층
전화 02-702-1724(기획편집) 02-703-1725(마케팅) 02-704-1724(경영지원)
팩스 02-703-2219
이메일 dasanbooks@hanmail.net
홈페이지 www.dasanbooks.com

출판등록 2005년 12월 23일 제313-2005-00277호

필름 출력 스크린그래픽센타 종이 월드페이퍼(주) 인쇄·제본 (주)현문

ISBN 978-89-6370-450-0 14740
SET 978-89-6370-438-8

who?

*Marie
Curie*

마리 퀴리

글 **이숙자** | 그림 **스튜디오 청비** | 번역 **자넷 재완 신** | 감수 **김수희**

Dasan Kid

Marie Curie

Polish scientist, November 7, 1867 ~ July 4, 1934

Marie Curie was the scientist who opened the doors to nuclear physics. She was born in Poland, a colony of Russia at the time. Instead of learning the Polish language, she had to learn Russian and Russian history. Having grown up under Russian colonization without being able to use her native tongue freely, Curie never lost her love for her motherland throughout her whole life.

Marie, who was very bright, wanted to study in college but because of her lack of resources had to get a job first. She helped to support her sister's medical studies first and worked as a governess for eight years. After that, she was able to enter Sorbonne University. Living at her sister's house while attending university, Marie studied science and graduated at the top of her class.

After graduation, she began doing research on radioactive materials, about which little was known. No other scientists were interested in the research of a Polish immigrant woman who used to be a governess.

However, Curie persevered and continued her research. After years of laboring to break down tons of ore and separate its elements, she discovered a new radioactive element. She named the element after her motherland and called it polonium.

Later, she discovered another radioactive element, radium. Taking her husband's place, she became the first female professor at Sorbonne University and continued her research. Marie Curie's groundbreaking research opened the doors for nuclear physics and later, the nuclear physics field made incredible strides.

Curie was the first female scientist to receive the Nobel Prize and also the first scientist to receive two Nobel Prizes. Marie Curie is a role model for many young women who aspire not only to be scientists but also to change the world.

마리 퀴리

폴란드 태생의 과학자, 1867년 11월 7일 ~ 1934년 7월 4일

마리 퀴리는 핵물리학의 문을 연 과학자입니다. 마리 퀴리는 러시아의 지배를 받던 폴란드에서 태어났습니다. 어린 시절 마리는 폴란드어로 공부하는 대신 러시아어로 러시아 역사를 배워야 했습니다. 러시아의 지배 아래 폴란드어를 자유롭게 사용할 수 없었던 마리는 평생 조국에 대한 사랑을 잊지 않고 간직하게 됩니다.

총명했던 마리는 대학에서 진학하고 싶었지만 가난 때문에 먼저 돈부터 벌어야 했습니다. 그래서 의사가 되고 싶어 한 언니를 먼저 대학에 보내고 가정교사로 8년이나 일한 끝에 소르본 대학에 들어갈 수 있었습니다. 언니의 집에서 생활하며 마리는 소르본 대학을 수석으로 졸업합니다.

대학에서 과학을 전공한 마리는 졸업 후 당시 잘 알려져 있지 않았던 방사능 물질을 연구하기 시작합니다. 가정교사 출신 폴란드 이민자이자 여자, 한 남자의 아내인 마리의 연구에 관심을 갖는 과학자는 없었습니다.

하지만 마리는 포기하지 않고 연구를 계속했습니다. 몇 톤이나 하는 광석을 부수고 분리하는 몇 년간의 노동이 이어진 끝에 새로운 방사성 원소를 발견하게 되었습니다. 마리는 원소에 조국의 이름을 따 폴로늄이라 이름 붙였습니다.

이후 마리는 또 하나의 방사능 물질 라듐을 발견합니다. 마리는 남편의 뒤를 이어 소르본 대학 최초의 여자 교수가 되었고 연구를 계속했습니다. 마리의 연구는 핵물리학의 문을 연 획기적인 내용을 담고 있었고 이후 핵물리학 분야는 눈부신 발전을 하게 됩니다.

마리 퀴리는 노벨상을 수상한 최초의 여성 과학자이자 노벨상을 두 번 수상한 최초의 과학자로 과학자를 꿈꾸는 많은 여성들의 본보기가 되고 있습니다.

이 책을 만든 사람들

글 · 이숙자

만화 스토리 작가로 왕성하게 활동하고 있습니다. 지금까지 고전, 명작, 과학, 논술, 경제 등 다양한 분야의 학습 만화 작업을 해 왔습니다. 현재는 어린이들이 닮고 싶고, 되고 싶은 인물 이야기를 쓰는 데 열중하고 있습니다. (firemecca@hanmail.net)

그림 · 스튜디오 청비

기발한 상상력을 바탕으로 새롭고 재미있는 콘텐츠를 만들어 내는 만화 창작 집단입니다. 어린이들이 책을 읽고 큰 꿈을 품기를 바라는 마음으로 즐겁게 작업하고 있습니다. 작품으로 『성철 스님』, 『아 다르고 어 다른 우리말 101가지』, 『반기문 유엔 사무총장의 꿈과 도전』 등이 있습니다.

번역 · 자넷 재완 신(Janet Jaywan Shin)

미국 메릴랜드 주에서 태어나고 자랐습니다. 메릴랜드 대학교에서 언어학을 전공하고 UCLA에서 응용언어학 석사 학위를 취득했습니다. 서울대학교 언어교육원에서 전임 강사, 서울대학교 사범대학교 영어교육과에서 초빙교수로 일했습니다. 감수한 책으로 『서울대생한테 비밀 영어과외받기』가 있고 고등학교 영어 교과서 교정 작업에 참여했습니다.

감수 · 김수희

연세대학교에서 역사를 전공했습니다. 이후 한국뿐 아니라 일본, 미국에서 한국어, 일본어, 영어를 가르쳐 왔으며 부모를 위한 영어교육용 책을 썼습니다. 영어교육채널 EBSe '엄마표 영어특강'에서 강의를 하며 홈스쿨, 알파벳과 파닉스, 다차원 테마 영어 수업 기법을 알리고 있습니다. 전국 각지에서 어린이 영어 교육에 대한 강연을 하며 창의적이고 열정적인 교수법으로 영어를 배우고자 하는 어린이와 부모들에게 많은 도움을 주고 있습니다.

Marie Curie

Marie Curie discovered _____, which is a radioactive element, used in the treatment of _____.

a. radium, cancer
b. X-ray, cold
c. uranium, diabetes

Answer: a

Contents

01 A Bright Child from a Poor Family

Track 01 ▶

Marie Curie was born in 1867 in Warsaw, Poland, which was then part of the Russian Empire. Her original name was Marya Sklodowska.

What are all these things?

?

They're so shiny.

I wonder what they're used to hold.

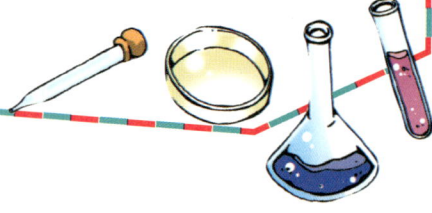

14

Papa, what are you going to do with these rocks?

Haha. You're so curious about everything, little Manya. The study of physics includes the study of different rocks like these.

What? You can study about rocks?

Manya, even these rocks are not meaningless things, You'll find out when you get older and study physics.

Study physics?

17

18

Then give me a kiss, Mama. Mmm~

No!

Manya, don't get too close!

She never kisses me.

Other mommies give kisses...

Does Mama not love me? I wish she'd kiss me just once...

Marie's mother suffered from tuberculosis so she never hugged or kissed her little daughter. To avoid spreading her illness, she would use her own dish and spoon.

Dear, now that my pay has increased, we'll be able to cure your illness soon. Stay strong.

Cough! Cough!

In 1868, the year after Marie was born, her father began working at a boys high school in Warsaw as both a physics teacher and vice-principal. He hoped that with a higher salary he could then afford to treat his wife's illness.

I feel sorry for the children. Manya's still a baby and I have yet to hold her in my arms.

Dear, are you alright?

Cough cough! Ugh!

Tuberculosis is a disease that is easily treatable today, but in the past, many people lost their lives due to tuberculosis. In place of their sick mother, Marie's second oldest sister Bronya would often play with Marie.

Now, repeat after the teacher.

Manya, you wanna play school?

Yeah!

Lo- looong... a-a-go... o-uuur...

couuun- trrry...

Sigh!

Tsk...

Teacher, I'll read it.

Long ago, our country was...

22

Marie continued to read a lot, without her mother's knowledge. Whenever she would concentrate on a book, Marie would be completely unaware of the chatter and things happening around her.

Scared ya, didn't we?

Manya!

Aaaaah!

...

She didn't even flinch!

Let's see if she can ignore this.

...

Heh heh. The moment she gets up from reading her book, she'll probably be so shocked she's gonna faint.

Boy, this is boring, waiting so long.

How much longer do we have to wait?

There! She's finally done reading! Any minute... heh heh!

BANG

Whoa.

02

The Sadness of Losing One's Homeland

 Track 10 ▶

There were many sad events during Marie's childhood. She coped with the sadness by delving deeper into books.

Look here, Mr. Sklodowski!

This student wrote his answer in Polish. How could you mark it correct?

This is not a test on the Russian language.

I marked it correct because he wrote the correct answer to the math problem.

Are you saying you will continue to break the school policy of teaching in Polish when they should be learning in Russian?

Sigh. It's unjust that we have lost our homeland, but on top of that, to not be able to teach our children our own language!

In 1873 when Marie was six years old, her father was fired from his vice-principal position and had to work as a regular teacher on half his original salary. Their family moved out of their house and into a more run-down place.

Sigh. This house is so old and shabby. How can we live in this dirty place?

There are people in worse situations, you all.

That's right. This is just temporary.

Russia is forcing us Poles to learn Russian history and Russian language, and trying to take away our people's spirit.

Yes, sir.

That's why all your school studies are in Russian. If they catch you studying Polish, they'll ship you away to Siberia.

I heard Siberia is so cold that people freeze to death there.

Russia is bad!

Right now, we have no choice but to learn Russian but it's a real insult to our pride.

Insult to our pride?

In addition, Marie's father who had a trusting personality ended up losing a large sum of money that he had invested into a crooked business. This made their financial situation even more difficult. Marie's parents decided to teach students in their home.

I have a good idea.

What is it?

Let's make our home a boarding home for students to live and also study here. We can make some money by providing room and board to them.

That'll probably interfere with your work...

Then one day, one of the boarders caught typhus, which spread to Marie's oldest two sisters, Zosia and Bronya.

Huff, huff

Now Zosia and Bronya are sick too, along with Mama.

Manya, here you are.

Bronya's fever has gone down quite a bit.

Ohhh, I'm so cold.

But why is Zosia getting worse?

Sobbb...

Now, let's all say our final goodbyes to Zosia.

Bronya was able to recover, but Zosia succumbed to typhus and died at the age of twelve.

However, in May 1878, when Marie was eleven years old, her mother passed away.

Bronya, now that you're the oldest, you're going to have to take care of a lot of the housework. And Hella, you'll be able to help Bronya, won't you?

Mama, no! Waah!

Joseph, you said you wanted to become a doctor so keep studying hard.

Mother!

Manya, I am the most sorry to you. I've never even been able to kiss you even once.

Mama, it's okay.

You don't have to give me a kiss. Just don't go. Sobbb!

After her mother passed away, Marie tried to distract herself from the pain by concentrating on her studies. Marie was one or two years younger than her classmates but she surpassed them in her studies.

36

And why aren't they studying Russian?

These girls will eventually have to do housework, so learning to sew is a necessary skill.

That is true. But I need to see for myself whether they are learning the Russian language and culture properly. Please choose one student.

It's my turn.

Marya Sklodowska.

Yes.

Marya, who is the current Russian czar ruling over us?

It's...

03

Working as a Governess

CD1 Track 17 ▶

In June, 1883, 16-year-old Marie graduated at the top of her class at Warsaw Public High School, but she couldn't attend university. Their family was poor, but also at the time, universities in Poland did not admit female students.

Yuck, I don't ever want to look at a Russian dictionary again!

Marya, congratulations on graduating valedictorian of the class. What's wrong? You look down.

Actually,

I don't know what to do with myself now.

Ever since she was young, Marie dreamed of studying physics and becoming a physicist.

But the only way girls can take university classes is to study abroad.

I know. It's so unfair that only boys can go to university in Poland!

Papa, Zosia's just sleeping, right?

You don't have to give me a kiss. Just don't go.

Sigh. But there's no way I can go with only this much. At this rate, I won't ever be able to study abroad!

I hope you can somehow go abroad soon.

One day...

Bronya!

Whew, let me catch my breath. Bronya, go to Paris now!

What?

While you're studying, I'll work and send you tuition money.

How in the world are you going to earn money?

Marie told her that she would become a governess and send half of her paycheck to Bronya. In exchange, when Bronya finished her studies and became a doctor, she could pay Marie's tuition.

What do you think? Good idea, huh?

If it weren't for Marie's idea and determination, the dreams of the two sisters, a future doctor and scientist, might never have been fulfilled.

I just learned how to read while we were playing school!

Marya, you've been the smart one ever since you were a child. You should go to Paris first.

No, you have to go first. It's okay.

I'm only seventeen, but you'll be twenty soon, so you shouldn't delay much longer.

And it's natural for the older sister to go first anyway.

Marya.

46

Marie began working as a governess in the home of a wealthy family in Warsaw. And whenever she wasn't teaching the children, she would borrow books on math and physics from the library and study on her own.

Marya, could you wait a little longer for this month's pay?

I'll be sure to give it to you next month.

Yes, that's alright, madame.

They live extravagantly with every possible luxury but they don't want to spend the small amount for a governess' pay.

I've been waiting for so long... what should I do about the tuition I need to send Bronya now?

We need to use fuel sparingly but you have it lit until this late at night.

Oh, I'm sorry. I didn't realize how time had passed while I was studying.

Tsk. This isn't the first time this has happened.

I can handle everything else, but I can't stand being kept from studying!

In 1886, 19-year-old Marie moved far from Warsaw to a remote town called Szczuki to work as a governess in a new home.

I can send Bronya more money now since they'll give me 500 rubles a year with free room and board.

Szczuki was a factory town with black chimney smoke filling the skies. The family Marie was to work for ran a factory that processed sugar beets into sugar.

You've come a long way. These are our children you will be teaching.

My name is Bronka. I'm nineteen.

Nice to meet you. We're the same age, so I hope we can be friends.

My sister Andzia is ten, but she likes to play a lot so you're going to have a hard time teaching her.

Marie saw children of factory workers there who were filthy and dressed in rags.

Andzia, it's time to study but where have you gone?

I don't think she's here. She might have gone to watch the sugar beet harvesting so let's check there.

How can they play outside all day? Is it because their parents aren't around to watch them and they can't go to school?

These children's parents couldn't take care of them because they had to work at the factory from early morning until late in the evening. Furthermore, they couldn't send them to school because they were poor.

Bronka, I'm going to teach those children Polish!

Marya, if you get caught you could get shipped off to Siberia.

Those kids are going to be the leaders of Poland in the future. So they need to know our language and how to write. Bronka, you're going to help me, aren't you?

Alright, Marya. But we've got to be careful not to get caught.

Marie began to secretly teach the village children in a back room of Bronka's house. And after a day's work, she would reduce her sleeping hours and study late into the night.

If you all don't know the Polish language or history, then Poland can never have a promising future.

My writing is so crooked. Studying is much harder than picking sugar beets.

Can you teach us how to read and write, too? I was amazed to see my child writing his name all by himself.

Of course, anytime.

Children need to be educated in order for a better world to be created.

My dear sister Bronya, I think that one needs to work hard in order to create a better future for oneself. I'm currently studying the subjects I will need to know by the time you come to get me.

Father continues to send me math problems to solve and tells me that I must not be lazy in my studies if I want to succeed in life.

Then around this time, Marie experiences a major heartbreak when the oldest son of the family returns home from college in Warsaw.

I'm surprised to meet a girl who likes math and science like you. Most girls find them to be difficult.

I think of you as my lifelong soulmate, Marya.

What? You want to marry a penniless girl who lives in someone else's house as a governess?

In the spring of 1889, Marie visited her father on the way to transferring to a different city. Her father had become the principal of a school on the outskirts of Warsaw, so his financial situation had improved.

Father has aged so much in the last few years!

The wrinkles in his forehead have gotten deeper and his hair has gone completely white!

Marya must be going through a lot. She doesn't look well!

Being a principal is much harder than being a teacher, isn't it?

The work is not that hard. I am more worried about you.

I didn't think Father would age this quickly. He will only continue to grow older and get weaker.

I'm worried about when I will have to go to Paris and leave Father.

When will Bronya call for me to come join her? I'm already 22 now.

Marie's new mistress liked to bring her along to fancy parties and gatherings. But Marie had no interest in these events whatsoever.

Haha! Hoho!

I always feel awkward and uncomfortable in these settings.

Our governess was valedictorian of her graduating class at Warsaw Public High School. She always has a book in her hand.

55

After I send half of my pay to Bronya, I don't have enough money to buy new clothes or dress stylishly.

But even if I did have enough money, I would probably still dress the same. After all, being absorbed in a book is what makes me happiest.

Extravagance and vanity just don't suit me!

But what's the use of gaining all this knowledge from books? I don't even have a laboratory to test out this information...

After quitting her work as a governess, Marie returned to Warsaw and was able to concentrate for a while on the studies that she enjoyed. She was able to use a laboratory in the Museum of Industry and Agriculture, thanks to her cousin who was the manager.

Marya, I'll let you satisfy the passion you have for science as much as you like.

Experiments are really fun.

I can actually use the science laboratory equipment that Father had introduced to me when I was a child!

They're so shiny.

Wow, amazing! Just like in the books, a chemical reaction occurred.

58

No matter how hard she tried though, the results did not always turn out the way it indicated in the textbooks. But Marie became certain that physics and chemistry research were the fields that best suited her.

...

I can't wait for the day when I'll be able to research and experiment as much as I want to in college.

To imagine myself attending Sorbonne University in Paris, where world-renowned scholars are gathered!

Dear Bronya, When do you think I can go to Paris? Several years have passed already since I had decided to study abroad. If you can just give me room and board, I want to go to Paris.

04 Sorbonne's Eccentric Coed

 Track 26 ▶

Dear Marya,
It's already been eight long years since you graduated from high school. It's been a hard life, hasn't it? Thanks to you, I've been able to graduate and become a doctor.

Bronya, I'm so proud of you.

I have not forgotten the agreement we made. Now it's my turn to help you. Marya, come stay at our house in Paris while you study here.

In November, 1891, 24-year-old Marie left to study abroad at the school she had dreamed so much about, Sorbonne University. In order to save every penny, she took all of her belongings with her instead of shipping them. And then she bought the cheapest train ticket for a fourth class seat and left for Paris.

Once I finish my studies, I will return to Warsaw and teach Polish students, just like Father. And I will live together with Father.

There was soon a rumor that an eccentric female student had enrolled at Sorbonne University.

Today's lesson is...

What? It's her again. She always comes early to class, sits in the front row and studies like that.

That's Marie, the curly blond from Poland, right?

Her name is Marie?

She had changed her name to Marie, the French version of Marya. At school, the library was Marie's favorite place to go and the laboratory was the place she loved the most.

I went through so much to get here. I don't want to spend my college life like any other student.

61

Science is the very study of unraveling the mysteries of nature. Discovering the ruling principles which govern the universe is what science is about.

Science is the very study of unraveling the mysteries of nature...

While Marie was attending Sorbonne University, there were only 23 female students out of a total of 1,825 students. There were even fewer female students in the science departments.

Hey, Marie! Do you want to go see the Eiffel Tower?

Sorry. I'm heading to the library.

Marie, you have to take a break and cool your head once in a while.

If you've come to Paris, you have to see the Eiffel Tower. Or how about going to the beautiful Seine River?

Just because I'm attending university doesn't mean that I get more respect as a woman.

Marie wanted to prove to them that their thinking was wrong.

Just wait and see. I'll graduate number one from Sorbonne and become a competent scientist!

But even though she studied in her free time while she was a governess, it wasn't easy to take university classes in French.

When the professor speaks quickly, there are so many parts that I don't understand.

I've got to first become more fluent in French.

Marie was living at her sister's house while she took classes. By this time Bronya had married a fellow Polish doctor named Dluski.

Marie, you study late into the night even at home?

65

...

Sigh. Even when she was young, she would be completely unaware of anything around her when she was reading!

Well, we can't help it if she's passionate about studying. Why don't you just make sure she eats properly?

Scholars and artists who were in exile from Poland often came to visit the Dluski home. This didn't help Marie's French studies very much.

This house is like the Polish boat that brought Poles out of the motherland!

Hahaha!

It's too hard to study here in this house.

Marie moved to an attic room at the top of an old rundown six-story building. It was only ten minutes from Sorbonne University.

CREAK

CREAK

This is great. Before, I would still be sitting on a bus on my way home, but now I can be reading.

Oh no, there's no more coal to put in the furnace.

The cheap attic room which cost 25 francs a month had no heating and terrible conditions. However, Marie was more content now than at any other time in her life.

I'm wearing every piece of clothing I own right now, and I'm so cold I can't stand it.

But I love the fact that there is nothing here to distract me so I can fully concentrate on my studying!

I miss Father!

Oh!

Marie, who would often skip meals to save time and money by not cooking or buying food, eventually collapsed.

It's obvious. You've been studying so hard you haven't been eating properly.

Poor Marie.

Let's prepare some steak and potatoes so that Marie can regain her strength.

I don't understand why she's sacrificing her life for her studies... Her grades are fine. What's wrong with resting once in a while?

Marie, you get out of that attic room at once, and come back and live with us!

70

However, after being cared for by her sister, Marie regained her strength and returned to her attic room.

Sorry, Bronya.

I've waited so long to come to Paris. If I give up now, all of my preparations will go to waste.

And more than anything else, when I think of Father back in Poland, I am reminded that I mustn't dawdle in my studies.

Marie's efforts did not go to waste. After just a year and a half in Paris, Marie graduated with a physics degree at the top of the class. Exactly ten years had passed since she had graduated from Warsaw Public High School.

Marie, that's amazing! Out of all the smart young people from all over the world at Sorbonne, you came in first place!

Yeah, I guess it's a start.

So now you're going back to Warsaw to become a teacher, aren't you?

No, I want to further study mathematics at Sorbonne.

What? You want to put yourself through more suffering?

But in order for me to study more, I've got to work for five years as a governess to save up for my tuition.

Fortunately, Marie received a scholarship for foreign students from the French government called the Alexandrovitch Scholarship and began studying for the mathematics entrance exam.

The scholarship will cover the tuition, but what do I do for my living expenses?

Hey, Sorbonne's eccentric coed!

Oh, Professor Lippman!

How is your studying going for the math entrance exam?

Professor Lippman was approached by the Society for the Encouragement of National Industry to research the magnetic property* of various metals, and he, in turn, asked Marie to head up the project.

Wow, thank you so much, Professor. Now I won't have to worry about how to pay for my living expenses.

Haha. It's not easy to find such outstanding students like you.

Soon afterwards, Marie began research on the magnetic property of metals, using Professor Lippman's laboratory. However there were many difficulties in the research because the lab was too small to conduct the experiments. Then one day, Marie was introduced to a scientist who was able to provide some help.

I heard that you are doing research on the magnetic property of metals.

Yes, that's right.

But that kind of research is probably difficult to conduct in a university laboratory, isn't it?

Right. To gather many metals and analyze their magnetic qualities, the right equipment and a proper place are necessary. But it's quite difficult to do this in Professor Lippman's laboratory.

Hmm, in that case, let me introduce you to a researcher who can help you.

*magnetic property: Various properties that are displayed by magnetic objects.

One spring day in April, 1894, 29-year-old Marie met a 35-year-old French scientist named Pierre Curie. At the time, Curie was quite well-known for his outstanding research in the science field.

!

Pierre, this is the very girl who graduated from Sorbonne number one in the physics department.

Marie, Pierre is another person like you who thinks of nothing but experiments and research.

So, Marie, you're doing experiments on the magnetism of metals?

Yes. When metals encounter a magnetic force, they often break down, so I'm researching a way to prevent that from happening.

As Marie and Pierre spent more time together, they realized how much they had in common. Both had a very strong passion for science, but little interest in worldly success or fame.

I always thought a woman would only hinder my research...

After meeting Marie though, I realize my thinking has been wrong.

Pierre realized that the only woman who could walk together with him on the lonely and difficult path of science was Marie.

Come in, Pierre.

Oh, to think that Marie has been living in such poverty!

77

In July, 1894, Marie graduated with a masters degree in mathematics and returned to Warsaw, leaving Pierre broken-hearted.

I've always thought of women and love as useless things that only hinder my research, but...

But now if Marie is not by my side, I cannot do anything.

Ah, what if Marie never returns?

Dear Marie,
I know how much you love Poland. But knowing your endless passion for science, I hope that you will come back to Paris.

Pierre understood Marie well, and she finally opened her heart to his affections.

My loving Marie,
Can't we fulfill our dreams of science together?

05 The Scientist Couple

CD2 Track 01 ▶

On July 26, 1895, Marie and Pierre Curie had a simple wedding ceremony on a beautiful sunny day, and rode off on two bicycles for their honeymoon.

Pierre, this is so fun riding bicycles.

Haha. I knew you'd like it.

What? What did you say?

But actually, I already want to go back to the laboratory.

Hoho. Actually, I do too!

Haha!

80

After spending the whole summer visiting different places all around France by bicycle, they returned to Paris and got a small apartment near school. Pierre Curie taught students at the School of Physics and Chemistry (EPCI) as a professor.

I love the green garden and the sunlight that comes in through the windows.

But we only have a desk and a chair for furniture. Why don't we buy several more pieces of furniture?

No. If we increase our possessions, then the housework will also increase. I won't have a lot of time to do housework.

When I lived by myself, I didn't think it was a big deal to skip meals so that I could study more. Wow, cooking is really difficult.

How does it taste? I tried hard, but I don't naturally cook very well.

Whatever you make tastes great.

At the time, it was customary for women to do the housework. Marie Curie had a hard time juggling housework and studies, but she managed to pass the secondary school teacher's exam with the highest score. In addition, she began preparing for doctoral studies at Sorbonne.

Pierre, what did we eat for dinner tonight?

Well, I can't remember if we ate dinner tonight or not.

On September 12, 1897, Marie gave birth to her first daughter, Irene. Soon afterwards, Pierre Curie's mother passed away and his father, Dr. Eugene Curie, came to live with them.

Marie, what are you writing so diligently?

I'm recording Irene's growth details like her head circumference, weight, particular traits, and changes in movement.

Hahaha. Whatever you do, you do it like a scientist.

Waaah!

Come here, Irene.

Marie, I'll take care of Irene from now on. You can rest assured and prepare your doctoral dissertation.

Pierre didn't want Marie to give up her research because of their child. Fortunately, Marie's father-in-law was able to watch the baby so that she could continue her research.

Good Irene. Mama's busy so let's play with Grandpa.

He loves his granddaughter so much, I know he's going to take good care of her.

Marie began to look for a subject for her doctoral research. At that time, there were no women who had earned a doctoral degree for science at any university.

What would be a good topic for my dissertation?

Roentgen's X-ray?

Around that time, the discovery of the 'X-ray' by German physicist Wilhelm Roentgen was major news among scientists in 1895. Roentgen discovered a strange light that was invisible to the human eye but could penetrate the body. He named it 'X-ray' to signify that it was an "unknowable light."

Wow, this is really interesting!

I took an X-ray picture of my wife's hand and the bones of her hand are visible!

The X-rays penetrate a person's skin but not the bones. That's why the photograph turns out like this!

The X-ray brought about a groundbreaking advancement in the medical world, and scientists around the world worked to discover the secret of the X-ray. In 1896, a French scientist named Henri Becquerel discovered that a material called uranium similarly emitted an invisible light like an X-ray. He presented the results of his discovery in a scientific journal.

Minerals that contain uranium emit light onto phototype even in dark places where no light is present. However I don't know the reason for this.

- *Excerpt from Becquerel's article*

What? Uranium emits its own light?

Pierre, there's an astounding article in this scientific journal!

You mean Becquerel's discovery? I read that too and thought it was an astounding discovery myself.

This is an incredibly huge discovery! How does uranium emit rays without first absorbing light from the sun or other source?

The scientists of that time were so busy researching the X-ray that they didn't pay much attention to Becquerel's paper. But Curie intuitively knew how fascinating and incredible this discovery was.

She decided to write her doctoral dissertation on the rays emitted from the element uranium.

Marie, I know you're going to get good results from your research.

But I think I'm going to need a separate laboratory.

The laboratory that you and I share is too small.

I'll ask our school principal about it and find a laboratory for you.

Marie began conducting research in an old storage closet in the garden of the School of Physics and Chemistry where her husband worked.

But the floor of the laboratory was not finished and the roof was shoddy, leaking on rainy days.

Oh no. Now that I look at it again, this lab is in terrible shape.

If I can just do my experiments, any place is fine with me. I'm going to start my research immediately.

I'll improve the device I invented and build other equipment that you will need.

Marie tested other materials to see if any of them emitted rays like uranium using the Curie electrometer*. The electrometer that Pierre Curie invented could measure even very weak electrical currents.

Whew, this is harder than trying to find a needle in a haystack. Will I be able to find another element that emits light spontaneously like uranium?

After repeating the experiment thousands of times, Curie discovered the fact that thorium emits rays like uranium.

As I expected, there is another element that emits light like uranium!

Congratulations, Marie. I knew you could do it.

Curie coined the term radioactivity* for the phenomenon of materials like uranium and thorium emitting rays. But soon afterwards, she discovered something even more surprising.

Look at this light, Pierre!

*electrometer: An instrument which measures electricity or the change in electricity between charged objects.
*radioactivity: The property or action of releasing radiation as the nucleus of elements such as radium, uranium, and thorium break down.

Isn't that pitchblende* with the uranium removed?

While Marie was investigating ores that contained uranium and thorium and measuring the intensity of their radiation using the Curie electrometer, she discovered that a mineral called pitchblende gushed out a much stronger radiation than uranium or thorium.

Even when the uranium was removed from pitchblende, it still emitted a stronger radiation than uranium. Marie believed the source was another unknown element.

Pierre, there's a new element that we don't know about, which hasn't been discovered yet!

And this new element has a much stronger level of radioactivity than uranium or thorium!

Oh, that's an incredible discovery, Marie. I wonder what element it will be.

Marie investigated all elements, pure elements and compounds together. In 1898, she proposed a hypothesis that a few minerals emitted stronger radiation than pure uranium. She also wrote a paper explaining how measuring radiation is a method for discovering new elements.

*pitchblende: a major ore of pitch uranium, radium and uranium, which contains no crystals and is lump-shaped

I have established the hypothesis that the mineral pitchblende possesses a small amount of material which has a much greater radioactivity than uranium or thorium. This material will not be a known element. The reason is because I have already tested all of the known elements... The new radioactive material is chemically a new element. And radioactivity is the atom's innate characteristic.

- *Marie Curie's laboratory note*

Marie's advisor at Sorbonne, Gabriel Lippman, read her paper at the Academy of the Sciences. This paper contained two revolutionary research results. The first was that a new element could be discovered by the measurement of radioactivity. And the second was the assertion that radioactivity was an inherent characteristic of the atom.

What? Radioactivity, an inherent characteristic of the atom?

Does that make any sense? It's evident that this study was done incorrectly.

Scientists in those days believed that the atom was the smallest unit of matter. Marie believed that as well, so she thought that radioactivity was a characteristic of the atom. Later, the Curie couple conducted experiments to show that radioactivity originated from outside the atom, rather than from within. The fact that a particle smaller than the atom, the electron, exists will be discovered later by British physicist J.J. Thompson in 1897.

In order to separate the elements in pitchblende one by one, the mineral had to be broken down into small pieces and boiled until it was completely melted. Afterwards, the solution needed to be cooled little by little.

CLANK

CLANK

The elements could be separated because the lighter materials would crystallize first as the solution cooled.

Hmm! These crystals are the very elements that make up pitchblende.

But all of the elements cannot be separated the first time, so we need to repeat this process several times.

Ah, this time the crystals did not form the way they're supposed to! And last time, the experiment was ruined because some foreign substance got mixed in!

Sigh! We have no choice but to start back at square one.

Curie needed to separate out each of the elements of pitchblende, which was composed of about thirty chemical substances. Then each separated crystal needed to be tested one by one for radioactivity, and the nonradioactive ones were removed. Then among the crystals found to be radioactive, the ones with uranium or thorium were also removed.

Oh no!

Oh no. Rain is getting into the experiment equipment!

We've got to move it to where the rain isn't seeping in!

Sigh. When do you think we can have a good research laboratory where we can fully concentrate on our research?

We'd better wait until the rain stops.

PATTER

PITTER

Their research conditions weren't very good but the Curies did not give up. In July, 1898, Marie Curie finally found the substance that was more radioactive than uranium.

Look, Pierre! The light from this substance is much stronger than uranium!

On December 19, 1898, Marie found another element. Only one year since she began her research on uranium, she made a great discovery which would astonish the world.

My goodness, Pierre! This time it's an element that has 900 times the radioactivity of uranium!

I'll name this element 'radium.'

Marie, I'll present this at once to the Academy of the Sciences.

The Curies and chemist Gustave Bemont both presented papers about a new and strongly radioactive substance called radium, found in pitchblende. For the next ten years, scientists discovered more about the atom and its structure than had been discovered in all of the past years put together.

As expected, however, there were a number of chemists who did not recognize the discovery of the new element.

If there really is radium hidden in pitchblende ore, then separate it out and show it to me.

I won't believe it until I see the actual substance with my own eyes, touch it, and measure its weight.

Physicists acknowledged the Curies' research results, but chemists couldn't believe that radium existed without seeing it for themselves.

The only work Marie had left to do was to extract pure radium. But she didn't realize then just how gigantic a task that was.

You want to move your research laboratory?

Yes, sir. The storage room we're using now doesn't have a finished floor and the roof is leaky. How can we continue to do experiments there?

Well, then there's a barn across from the storage room that isn't being used. You can use that instead.

Oh my, this is worse than the storage room we're using now.

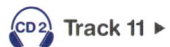

The students used to have anatomy class here. The roof leaks and it's filled with dust, so they moved the cadavers somewhere else.

But I like the spacious yard.

Marie Curie began her work extracting pure radium from substances containing radium.

Then I'll use all of our savings to buy some pitchblende.

Maire would stir the pot of solution all day with a metal rod that was taller than herself, and distill* the solution.

We still have a long way to go before we get pure radium. We expected it to be difficult, but not this difficult.

*distill: To heat a solution, cool the gas which forms, and make it into a solution again. A component from a mixture can be isolated by utilizing the difference in boiling points of each component.

Whew. In order to extract enough radium for the eye to see, we would need to melt an incredible amount of pitchblende, wouldn't we?

That's right.

But the Curies did not have enough money to buy that huge quantity of pitchblende.

What should we do?

Aha! Uranium is mined from pitchblende. Perhaps we can obtain the leftover pitchblende after the uranium has been removed.

Pierre Curie found out that they stored the remaining pitchblende, from which the uranium had been extracted, in the woods. He was able to obtain a large heap of pitchblende from the Austrian government for free.

The pitchblende we've been waiting for is finally here.

Ah, my dear baby, radium, is inside, isn't it?

From this point on, the Curies decided to divide up the work. Marie would extract the radium and Pierre would examine the extraction for radium's properties.

If we didn't have this large yard, we might not have had a place to store all of this pitchblende.

Marie melted the pitchblende one ton at a time. By doing this, she began to extract barium, a substance which contained radium.

Marie, this task is too difficult for you to do.

No, Pierre. You are better at using the delicate instruments. And you have to teach your classes and oversee research, so that doesn't leave you with much time. It's better if I do this work.

In the process of boiling the solution all day, Marie ruined her clothes and thick smoke and a toxic smell emanated continuously. The laboratory did not have good circulation. In the winter, it was freezing cold, and in the summer, it was suffocatingly hot.

A manual laborer probably doesn't have to work this hard. Marie, why don't you take a break from this for a while?

Pierre, I can't wait to see what radium will look like.

Well, I'm sure the color will be beautiful.

Pierre, I don't want to take a break. If I stop this work now, radium won't be able to be introduced to the world.

Can't you rest a bit until your health improves and start up again then?

You can quit. I'll just work by myself.

Marie was so exhausted some days that she would spill a distilled solution that she had been working on for months.

Sobb, I put so much work into this...

Marie, don't be too upset. There's plenty of pitchblende. And I'll finish up the work for today. Go on home and try to rest.

The search for pure radium continued for four years.

Is a laboratory supposed to be a sad and lonely place like this?

Tsk tsk. Even to a child, this laboratory looks shabby.

As the experiments continued, both Marie and Pierre Curie's health gradually grew worse. The reason was that when radiation penetrates a person's body, it reacts with the elements which compose the body and causes a change. At the time however, this fact was not known and the Curies conducted the experiments without proper clothes or even gloves.

My, this laboratory is so shoddy.

The Discovery of Radium

06

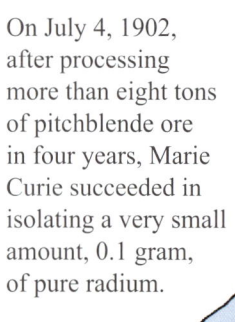

On July 4, 1902, after processing more than eight tons of pitchblende ore in four years, Marie Curie succeeded in isolating a very small amount, 0.1 gram, of pure radium.

It's close to becoming pure radium.

Ah, I wonder what color radium will be. I really want to see.

Ah, Pierre! It's pure radium! The radium is glowing by itself!

Oh, my dear baby, radium!

In December, 1903, Marie and Pierre Curie were credited with the discovery of radium and polonium. Together with Henri Becquerel, they received the world's most prestigious award, the Nobel Prize in Physics.

Wow, radium emits a bright blue light! It's truly a magical, marvelous light!

Marie Curie was the first woman to ever receive a Nobel Prize. And with the radium research, she was the first woman to ever receive a doctoral degree from Sorbonne University.

Marie, your body has gotten quite weak so we'd better postpone going to Sweden to receive the Nobel Prize.

Radium was an extremely significant discovery in history. It was a very useful substance to humanity. Scientists from various countries began to study radioactivity.

Pierre, your arm is so red!

I read a German scientist's research paper which stated that radium affected human cells, so I tested it on my own body.

Henri Becquerel also said that he got a serious burn on his chest after carrying radium around in his vest pocket.

If that's the case, then the radiation from radium could be effective in treating skin infections. I must test this out on animal subjects at once.

After the discovery of radium, many people thought that radiation therapy could be used effectively in hospitals. Pierre Curie continued to conduct experiments in order to develop radium into a medical tool. He and Marie hoped that the substance they discovered could be used in an advantageous way.

Hmm, radium is a useful substance to humans, but if exposed to too much, it can be dangerous.

As the therapeutic effects of radium became known, entrepreneurs thought hard about how to sell radium as a product. In the 1920s and 1930s, all kinds of quack radium products whose effects hadn't been tested were produced. They were incredibly popular and sold well.

This medicine which contains radium, for example, can easily treat rheumatism, even depression, all illnesses. It's a cure-all!

It contains radium? Then I'll take a bottle.

If it's radium medicine, then I'll buy a bottle, too.

If you use makeup containing radium, your face will become pretty and healthy. I have to buy one. I'm going to buy lipstick and bath soap with radium.

If you use hair cream containing radium, it'll preserve the curls in your hair for a long time?

Not only that, it reduces hair loss. And I heard that there's even a product that will restore the original color of white hair.

The radiation from radium can kill cancer cells, but there are also other side effects which occur. One American, who believed the advertisement that radium was good for one's health, drank a drink containing radium once a day for four years. In the end, his facial bones deteriorated and he suffered a painful death from bone cancer.

One day, Pierre Curie received a letter and became troubled. One American company wrote that if the Curies told them the method of extracting radium, they would pay them a large sum of money.

*extract: To take a substance out of a solid or liquid mixture.

Furthermore, radium is going to be used to treat illnesses. We must not commercialize it.

But think of all the suffering we've gone through.

Marie Curie thought of the past years which led up to the radium discovery. The Curies' greatest wish was to have a laboratory which had proper lab equipment and didn't leak whenever it rained.

The Curies however decided to unconditionally release all information about radium. They believed that scientific knowledge should be shared to benefit humanity.

The Nobel Prize and the prize money are all we need.

You're right, Marie.

Marie, I don't know why my body feels like this. My back pain is getting so bad that I can't sleep at night.

Marie and Pierre Curie were not in good health having done radiation research for so long. Pierre had once even deliberately exposed himself to radium's radiation and burned himself for the sake of research. Now he suffered from a mysterious pain for several days at a time.

Pierre, I won't be able to continue the research without you.

Don't think that way. Marie, whatever happens, you must continue the research.

A scientist has no right to abandon science.

Pierre's illness seems serious. The hospital doctors don't even know what it is.

Because of their poor health, the Curies weren't able to go to Stockholm, Sweden, for more than a year after they received the Nobel Prize. They went in 1905 to give an acceptance speech. Pierre spoke of several dangers of the misuse of radiation and some ways that it would benefit humanity.

In criminal hands, radium might become extremely dangerous.

Does humanity have anything to gain by learning the secrets of nature? Is humanity ready? Will it harm humanity? The powerful explosive that Alfred Nobel discovered is also a terrible means of destruction in the hands of the great criminals who lead the peoples towards war.

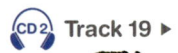

Oh my, look at Madame Curie's hands. They're rougher than men's hands. It must be from working with radium.

She doesn't even wear a simple ring. She really is as plain and simple as they say she is.

She is truly admirable.

And there is not a single jewel on her body.

Pierre, I'm worried that we won't be able to properly do research now that we're so well-known. We should go live in hiding somewhere that nobody knows about.

Haha. Then if scientists don't do research, then who will?

And the Curies seem to have such a good relationship. I envy them so much!

That afternoon, after having lunch with some professors and heading to his next appointment, Pierre Curie was hit by a passing stagecoach and died immediately. It was an unknown fact at the time, but his knees had gotten so damaged from radiation that he was visibly limping at the time he was hit by the carriage.

...

Marie Curie had gone out with Irene that day and when she returned around dusk, several Sorbonne professors were waiting for Marie with mournful faces.

My son is gone... how can this be?

The next morning, Marie saw the marigolds that her husband had brought home, still fresh on the kitchen table.

Pierre...

Pierre, I can't imagine being in this place by myself without you.

Newspapers all over the world reported Pierre Curie's death. Many people, including France's president, came to express their grievances to Madame Curie. Not long after his funeral, Curie's hair turned from a beautiful blond to gray.

In order to cope with her sadness, Maire plunged into her research all the more. That was her only way to cope with misfortune and sadness, ever since she was young. This is not unlike the way she dove into reading books after the deaths of her older sister and her mother.

Marie, a scientist has no right to abandon science. If a scientist doesn't do research, then who will?

123

07 The Final Struggle

CD2 Track 23 ▶

Marie Curie took her husband's position and became the first woman professor at Sorbonne. Her first lecture, which was several months after his death, was attended by hundreds of people who wanted to hear her lecture.

How could they give a woman the position of professor?

The time for that tradition to be done away with has arrived.

Madame Curie is the only person who possesses anywhere near the ability of Professor Curie and is capable of continuing the work that he was doing.

However it took two years before Maire became a regular professor. Sorbonne University had seven hundred years of tradition and custom during which women professors were not accepted.

Today is the day of Madame Curie's first lecture.

Ah, she's finally here!

When one considers the progress that has been made in physics in the past ten years, one is surprised at the advance that has taken place in our ideas concerning electricity and matter.

Pierre, I took your place in the lecture hall. I still cannot believe that you're no longer here, but for our children's sake I'm going to be strong.

Curie cared much about her daughters' education. She taught Irene, Eve, and the other professors' children with a few other Sorbonne professors.

Irene, look at this.

?

Wow, that's neat.

If you dip a wooden marble into ink and place it on a tilted surface, we can see that it rolls down making an arc shape.

No matter how much I read about it in the books, it's hard to understand. But you explain it in a way that's fun and easy!

Marie exposed Irene to a passion for science and a mindset for research. Irene would later marry a fellow scientist and together create artificial radiation, which would earn them a Nobel Prize in Chemistry.

126

Madame Curie also encouraged her daughters to be physically active, doing things like bicycling, swimming, hiking, and horseback riding. In addition, she taught them the Polish language, so that they wouldn't forget their homeland.

Irene is good at math and science, but what about you, Eve?

But, Mother, I'm better than Irene in music.

Marie's radioactivity research also continued. Working with one of Pierre Curie's students, Andre Louis Debierne, Maire succeeded in designing a method for measuring the quantity of pure radium and calculating the precise atomic weight of radium.

As a result, in 1911, Marie received her second Nobel Prize, this time in Chemistry, at the age of forty. This was the first time anyone had ever received two Nobel Prizes.

One day, a Polish scientist visited her laboratory to ask her to help start a radiation research institute in Warsaw.

I would love to work in Poland.

Unfortunately, Marie was already committed to establishing a joint research lab in conjunction with Sorbonne University and Pasteur Research Institute.

I'm sorry but I cannot break the commitment I have already made and go to Poland.

This was a chance for me to work in my homeland. It's too bad.

In July, 1914, two white buildings built for Paris' radioactivity research were completed. The building was named Radium Institute—Curie Building, and the street where the building was located was named Curie Street.

Pierre, it's already been eight years since you've left.

The Radium Institute is now completed so we have a good laboratory environment to freely do our work, but you aren't here.

But not long after the institute was established, Paris was invaded. Germany began attacking and France was soon engulfed in World War I. Research workers were drafted to serve on the battlefields, and large numbers of injured soldiers were brought daily to France's hospitals.

Ahhh!

It hurts so much. Argh!

Treatment would be much easier if we could take X-rays to see where the bullet entered the body or to see exactly where the injury is...

At the time, there were few hospitals equipped with X-ray equipment.

Marie Curie went from place to place to borrow X-ray machines to help save the lives of dying young soldiers.

To what do we owe the honor of a visit from the famous Marie Curie?

I would like to borrow your X-ray machine. I can return it to you at the end of the war.

Since you are using it for a good cause, of course you may borrow it, Dr. Curie.

After obtaining the X-ray machines, she recruited people among the professors and students who knew how to use the machines.

I'll help you too, Dr. Curie.

Me too. I'll help, too.

But there was often no electricity at the field hospitals*, where most of the injured soldiers were.

What do we do?

*field hospital: A temporary hospital set up near a battlefield equipped to provide remedial surgery and post-operative care.

Marie designed a way to use a small generator by connecting it to a car battery.

We can put the X-ray machine and the small generator in a car and transport it from place to place.

That's an excellent method, Madame Curie.

But in order to do that, many cars were necessary.

Are you going to go around and grovel again?

Why is Madame Curie at our house?

Marie went on another round of visits, this time to borrow cars.

How can I help?

Can you loan us your car? We'll return it to you after the war. We need to save the dying soldiers on the battlefield by taking the X-ray machine to them in a car.

Marie personally installed X-ray machines into 20 cars. She also persuaded the tight security to grant passes for the cars to travel to and from the battlefields. In addition, she secured medical certification so that they could be licensed to treat the wounded.

Here is the pass.

From this X-ray, it looks like the bullet is in between your ribs.

Dr. Curie, you should head home. It's quite late, so I'll drive you home.

Marie went around to hospitals to show doctors how to use the portable X-ray machines and took X-ray pictures of the wounded soldiers herself. When there were many wounded soldiers, sometimes she would spend days at a time amongst the wounded. Later, Marie's older daughter, Irene, also came to help. The French soldiers who were indebted to Marie's radiology car called it the "petite Curie."

Irene, hurry.

Yes, Mother.

More than one million X-rays were taken during the war. Around the time of the end of the war, there were about 200 hospitals that were equipped with X-ray machines.

On November 11, 1918, the war ended and France was completely free from the grips of the German soldiers. More than anything, Marie was overjoyed beyond words that Poland became an independent nation once again.

If Father were alive, how happy he would have been!

Using the Russian language is an insult to our pride!

Mother, I think we can reopen the Radium Institute now.

After the war ended, Marie Curie continued her radium research without rest. Her daughter, Irene, became her lab assistant and helped with her radioactivity research.

But the facility which was built right before the war was insufficient to conduct full research. One of the major problems was that they had only a very small amount of radium.

That American magazine keeps calling to interview you. What should I tell them?

How bothersome. Just tell them I'll do it.

Hello, Dr. Curie.

Around then, the editor-in-chief of a popular American magazine, Marie Maloney, came to meet Curie in order to interview her.

You have discovered radium and have been awarded not just one but two Nobel Prizes. We American women are very interested in you, Dr. Curie. That is why we want to interview you.

I heard that there is a lot of radium in America. My laboratory has barely one gram.

Marie Maloney was astonished by the fact that Marie Curie had barely one gram of radium. There were seven grams of radium in New York, and about 50 grams of radium nationwide in the States.

The person who discovered radium possesses only one gram of radium?

Yes, that's right. To tell you the truth, we don't have enough radium in our laboratory to do our research.

That is unbelievable.

After Marie Maloney returned to the States, she began a campaign to 'Send Madame Curie a Gram of Radium.' One gram of radium cost about $100,000, but this movement was very successful. They then invited her to come give a talk.

Mother, you're not well. Do you think you will be able to give a talk? Don't you think it might be too much for you?

If we want to receive the radium and continue our research, we must go.

I'm excited to be able to go to America. Irene, don't you like my outfit? The latest style is to wear a jacket with a gold pin fastened in the front.

Eve, it's not good to follow every trend to decorate your outer appearance. Look at Irene. She's always simple and plain.

So you mean I have to buy one outfit and wear it for the rest of my life, mending it until it wears out? Like you? No thank you.

Tsk tsk.

In May, 1921, when Marie Curie and her two daughters set sail and landed in New York, hundreds of people crowded the docks.

Amazing! Polish patriots, Girl Scouts, nurses and doctors, college students holding signs... all of these people came out to greet us!

Eve, not so loud!

137

Well, isn't this something?

Mother, I'm so fascinated by everything.

That girl's name is Eve, the girl with the radium eyes!

Please say a few words about receiving the gram of radium. What do you think is the reason American women gathered $100,000 on your behalf?

Marie, who preferred quiet affairs, would sit in a chair, looking at her feet, and calmly answer all the questions that were poured out at each interview.

Madame Curie, are you planning to visit the Grand Canyon?

Of course, you will attend the banquet that President Harding is hosting?

Marie Curie, with one gram of radium tightly wrapped in lead and placed in a brown box.

Here is the gram of radium. Many American women donated money to purchase this. It is the symbol of their gratitude and respect for the work that you have done as a woman scientist.

Thank you. Because of this gift, I can continue my research. But I will receive this gift not on behalf of myself, but on behalf of our research lab.

Eight years later, America donated another gram of radium to Curie, and she in turn gave it to the Radium Research Institute which was established in her homeland, Poland. From this point on, Marie put all of her energy into establishing research institutes around the world, for the sake of the next generation scientists.

In 1925, the Radium Institute of Warsaw was established in Poland for radium research.

Bronya, can you head up this laboratory?

It will be in good hands. But Marie, you don't look well. Take care of yourself.

Marie, who had done so much radiation research, didn't have a single part of her body that was healthy. She had cataract surgery for her eyes, she had severe ringing in her ears, and her hands were swollen and hurt from all the research that she could hardly move her fingers. Within her body, a large gallstone had formed and she was always suffering from an unexplainable exhaustion.

Irene, my fever is not getting better, so I'm going to head home.

I wonder what it is. There's never been an instance when she stopped her work because of illness.

Mother...

Doctors said that Curie had pernicious anemia and said it was probably due to the fact that she was exposed to radiation for a long time without proper protective gear. But that didn't stop Curie from continuing radiation research. That was the extent to which she loved radium.

Please take good care of these roses.

Why do her words sound so final?

From that day on, she was not able to go to the radium laboratory.

Marie Curie was seriously ill from the radium that she loved so much. Many people warned of the dangers of exposure to radium, but the Curies always kept radium salts in a glass bottle next to their bed. There were many times when Madame Curie would call radium "my child."

Irene, take my place and continue on with scientific research. Argh!

She's had a constant high fever and now she's lost her consciousness. Mother, Sobb!

Her hands are completely covered with burn scars from radium!

Mother, you mustn't go.

On July 4, 1934, Marie Curie passed away at Sancellemoz Hospice in Switzerland at the age of 67.

Marie, this is sand from Poland, the land you loved so much.

Mother!

In 1935, Curie's oldest daughter, Irene, and Irene's husband together discovered artificial radioactivity and received the Nobel Prize in Chemistry. Her younger daughter, Eve, wrote a biography of her mother's life and published it internationally. On April 20, 1995, Marie's body was relocated to the Pantheon*. She was the first woman to be buried at the Pantheon based on her own achievements.

*Pantheon: A national cemetery where France's national heroes are buried.

With the determination to do something that would help humanity, Marie Curie gave her life to the development of science. The first to discover the radioactive element, radium, she gave her life to the research of the properties of radioactive elements. And because of her outstanding research, Marie Curie became the first person to receive two Nobel Prizes. Not only that, she broke the tradition of an era when women could not become professors, and she became the first woman to earn her doctoral degree and the first woman professor. She influenced young girls around the world to fulfill their dream of becoming a scientist. Today there are many outstanding women scientists active in the field.

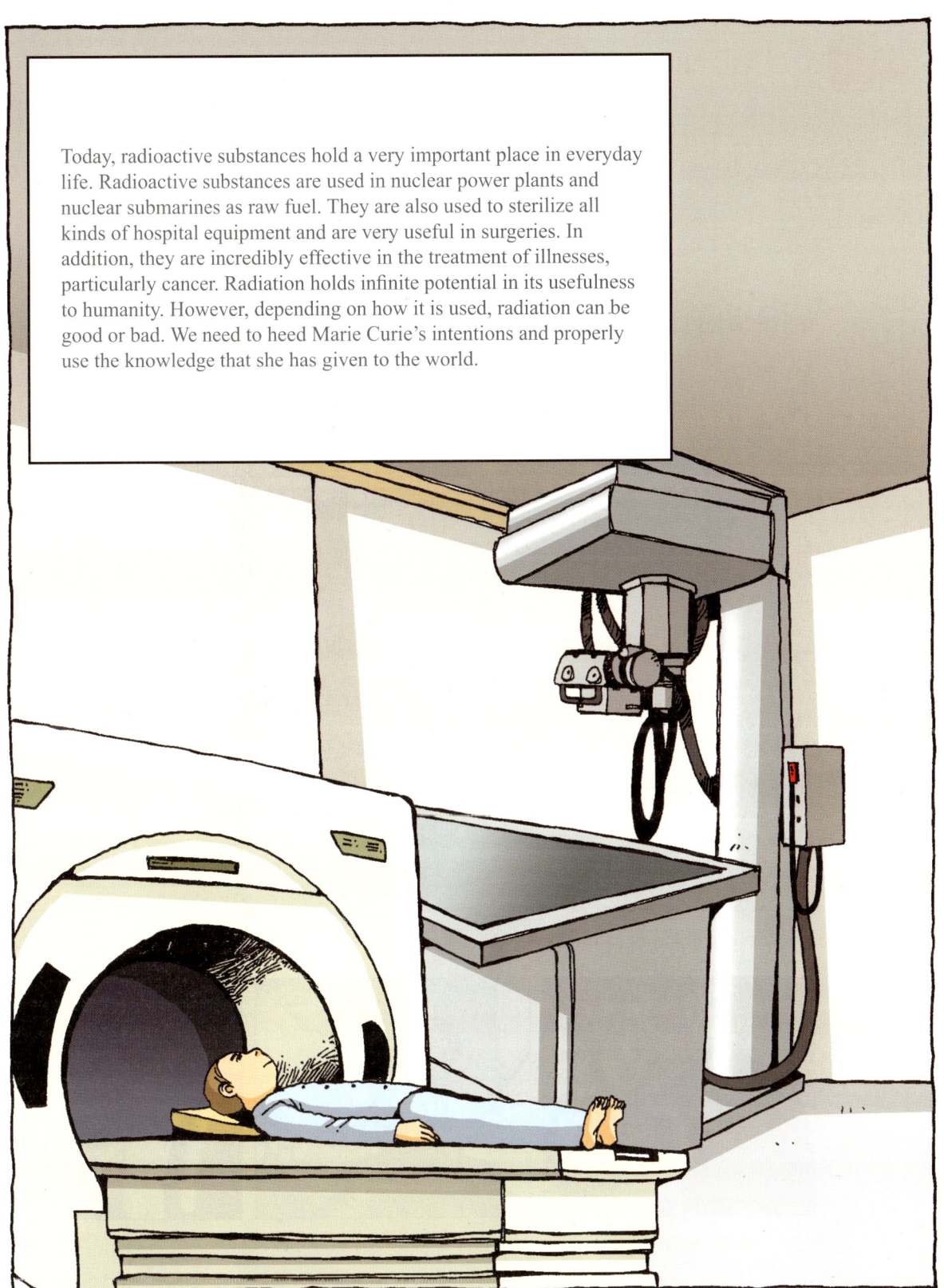

Today, radioactive substances hold a very important place in everyday life. Radioactive substances are used in nuclear power plants and nuclear submarines as raw fuel. They are also used to sterilize all kinds of hospital equipment and are very useful in surgeries. In addition, they are incredibly effective in the treatment of illnesses, particularly cancer. Radiation holds infinite potential in its usefulness to humanity. However, depending on how it is used, radiation can be good or bad. We need to heed Marie Curie's intentions and properly use the knowledge that she has given to the world.

Word Search

● Find the words which are hidden horizontally, vertically and diagonally.

```
C M Z G Q M Z G Q M Z G Q Q M Z G Q M X
W S C I E N T I S T N H W W N A H C N V
E B M J A B Q J E T E A R B A R I O B A
R V F P R D C K R V V K R R B C K M V L
E C U O A S E N T C H L T T R D U I C E
V X L Q Y N Z O Y X N Q Y Y O E N O X D
E Z F W U D I W C Z G W R U A V J N Z I
A N I E I A E O I A E P E I D R A E A C
L S L R C S G C N S L H H O S G S R S T
T D L U P O H T O D I Y O P D H T B D O
A F R Y H F E Y A T C S V A F U Y I F R
S G S U S T I D C R A I E I N G U T G I
T H S I D H M I D H L C R D H O I Y H A
O J A B S O R A F J T I F F J T J F J N
R K N P R O P O R M I A N A T E B G K I
H L A W K W A R D E Y N H H L E N H L B
J Q T M J Q T A U T C O R I T Y M J B L
L W E Q L W Y Q L W Y Q L L W Y Q L U E
Z W R E V E N T Z W K F Z Z S U F T J R
X E M E X M R I N C P O E T U R E X N M
W R E M O V E C P R O P H T R Q C I R P
```

scientist	valedictorian	fulfill	remove
physician	abroad	awkward	coed

Vocabulary

● Match each word to the correct meaning.

1. discover	• 물리학
2. research	• 학자
3. laboratory	• 발견하다
4. physics	• 실험
5. interest	• 수업료
6. governess	• 실험실
7. tuition	• 연구히디
8. poverty	• 흥미
9. experiment	• 뛰어난
10. scholar	• 별난, 괴짜인
11. eccentric	• 가정교사
12. outstanding	• 가난

Guess What?

● Guess what she said in the blank.

Isn't that pitchblende* with the uranium removed?

While Marie was investigating ores that contained uranium and thorium and measuring the intensity of their radiation using the Curie electrometer, she discovered that a mineral called pitchblende gushed out a much stronger radiation than uranium or thorium.

Even when the uranium was removed from pitchblende, it still emitted a stronger radiation than uranium. Marie believed the source was another unknown element.

And this new element has a much stronger level of radioactivity than uranium or thorium!

Oh, that's an incredible discovery, Marie. I wonder what element it will be.

Marie investigated all elements, pure elements and compounds together. In 1898, she proposed a hypothesis that a few minerals emitted stronger radiation than pure uranium. She also wrote a paper explaining how measuring radiation is a method for discovering new elements.

What X-ray Shows

During the first World War, Marie Curie decided to provide X-ray machines to help the wounded soldiers. She eventually designed the first mobile X-ray machine and got 20 cars equipped with the X-ray machines in order to travel along the battle fields during the war. She also trained 150 women to become X-ray technicians. Thanks to her, we can see our skeletons, and this is a picture of it.

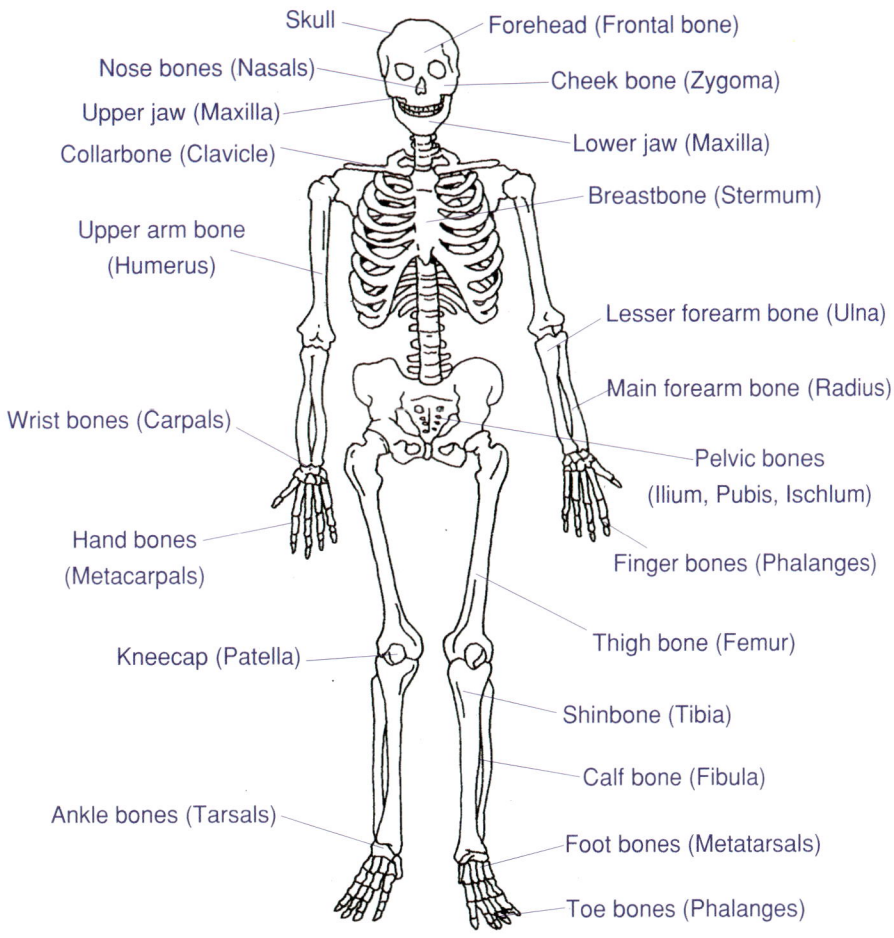

Skull
Forehead (Frontal bone)
Nose bones (Nasals)
Cheek bone (Zygoma)
Upper jaw (Maxilla)
Lower jaw (Maxilla)
Collarbone (Clavicle)
Breastbone (Sternum)
Upper arm bone (Humerus)
Lesser forearm bone (Ulna)
Main forearm bone (Radius)
Wrist bones (Carpals)
Pelvic bones (Ilium, Pubis, Ischlum)
Hand bones (Metacarpals)
Finger bones (Phalanges)
Thigh bone (Femur)
Kneecap (Patella)
Shinbone (Tibia)
Calf bone (Fibula)
Ankle bones (Tarsals)
Foot bones (Metatarsals)
Toe bones (Phalanges)

Lab Equipment

Marie Curie loved spending her time in the laboratory. These are the common equipment used in the chemistry lab, and are likely to have been used by Marie Curie for her experiments.

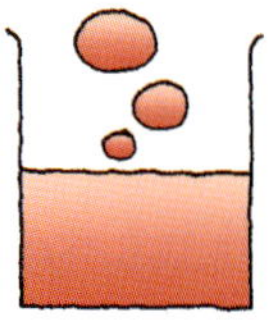

Beaker

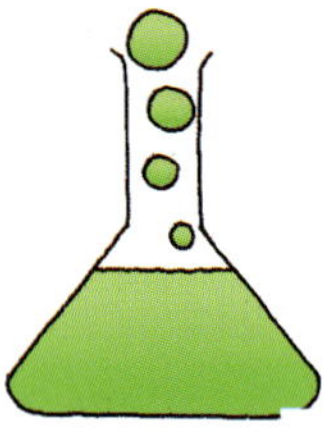

Flask

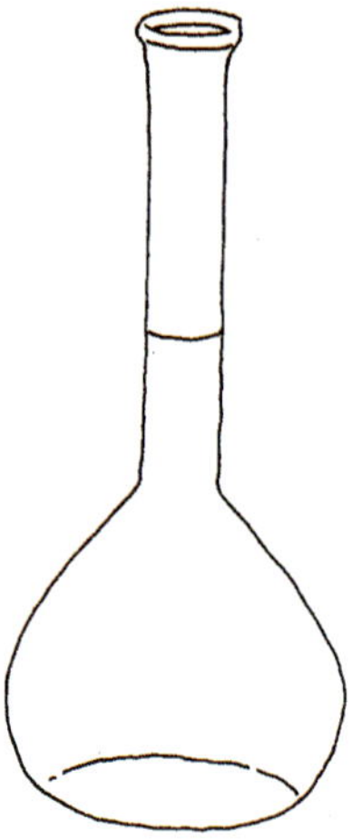

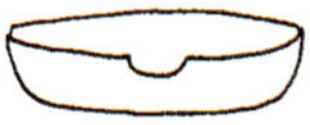

Evaporation dish

Volumetric flask

Erylenmeyer flask

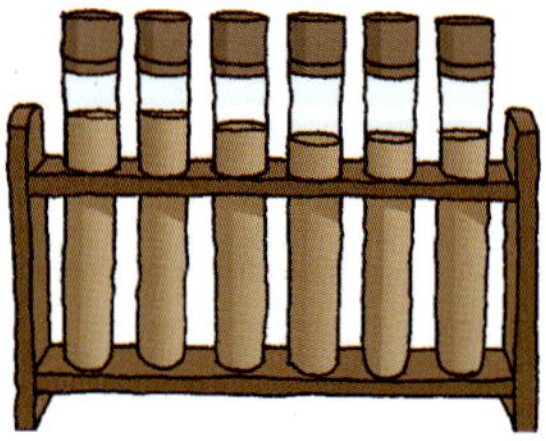

Test tube rack

dropper

Test tube holder

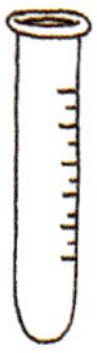

Test tube    Centrifuge tube

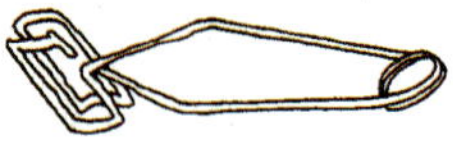

Test tube clamp

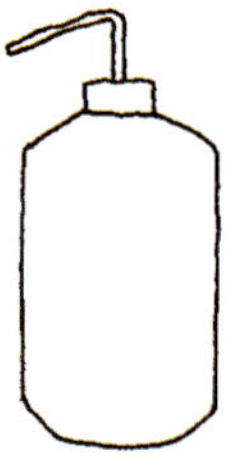

Distilled water bottle

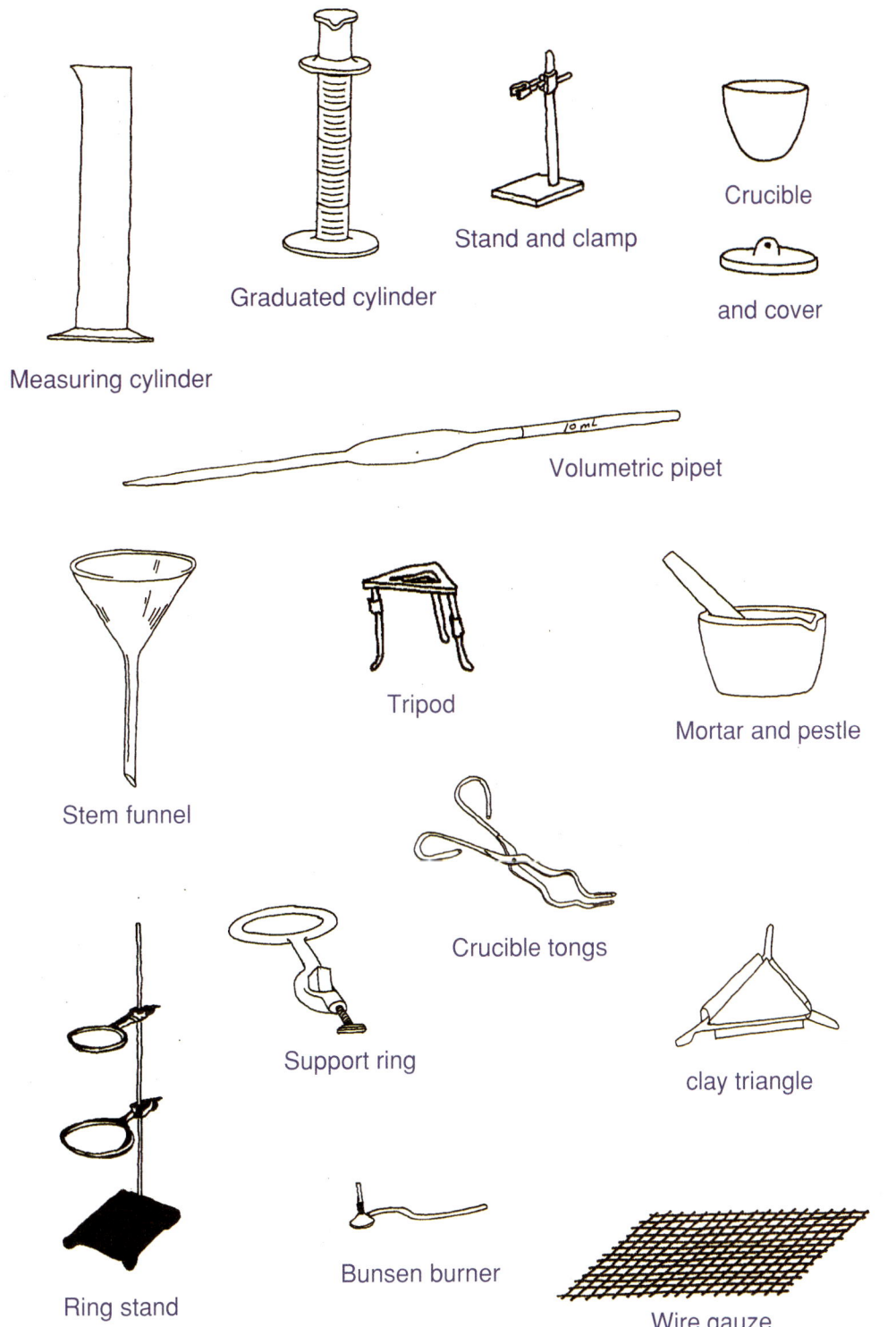

Graduated cylinder

Stand and clamp

Crucible

and cover

Measuring cylinder

Volumetric pipet

Tripod

Mortar and pestle

Stem funnel

Crucible tongs

Support ring

clay triangle

Ring stand

Bunsen burner

Wire gauze

연표

1867년 11월 7일, 폴란드 바르샤바에서 태어납니다.

1878년 11세 어머니가 결핵으로 세상을 떠납니다.

1891년 24세 소르본 대학에 들어갑니다.

1895년 28세 피에르 퀴리와 결혼합니다. 빌헬름 뢴트겐이 엑스선을 발견합니다.

1896년 29세 앙리 베크렐이 우라늄이 포함된 광석에서 인광 방출 현상(물체에 빛을 쬔 후 빛을 제거한 후에도 오랫동안 빛을 내는 현상)을 발견합니다.

1897년 30세 첫 딸 이렌 퀴리가 태어납니다.

1898년 31세 처음으로 '방사능'이라는 용어를 사용합니다. 우라늄보다 훨씬 강한 방사성 원소를 발견하여 폴로늄이라 이름 붙입니다. 12월, 새로운 방사성 원소를 발견하여 라듐이라는 이름을 붙입니다.

1902년 35세 순수한 라듐 0.1그램을 분리해냅니다.

1903년 36세 피에르 퀴리, 앙리 베크렐과 함께 방사능에 대한 연구로 노벨 물리학상을 공동 수상합니다.

1904년 37세	둘째 딸 에브 퀴리가 태어납니다.
1906년 39세	피에르 퀴리가 사고로 사망합니다. 소르본 대학 최초의 여성 교수가 됩니다.
1911년 44세	라듐과 폴로늄의 발견, 라듐의 분리를 인정받아 노벨 화학상을 받습니다. 노벨상을 두 번 받은 최초의 과학자가 됩니다.
1914년 47세	라듐 연구소를 엽니다.
1921년 54세	라듐 연구소에 필요한 라듐 구입 비용을 마련하기 위해 미국에서 모금 활동을 합니다.
1934년 67세	7월 4일, 악성 빈혈로 사망합니다. 딸 이렌과 사위 프레드리크 졸리오-퀴리가 인공 방사능을 발견합니다.
1995년	4월 20일, 프랑스의 국가적인 위인들이 묻혀 있는 국립묘지 팡테옹으로 이장됩니다. 자신의 업적만으로 팡테옹에 묻힌 최초의 여성이 됩니다.

Note

who? 01	Barack Obama	978-89-6370-514-9
who? 02	Charles Darwin	978-89-6370-515-6
who? 03	Bill Gates	978-89-6370-516-3
who? 04	Hillary Clinton	978-89-6370-517-0
who? 05	Stephen Hawking	978-89-6370-518-7
who? 06	Oprah Winfrey	978-89-6370-519-4
who? 07	Steven Spielberg	978-89-6370-520-0
who? 08	Thomas Edison	978-89-6370-521-7
who? 09	Abraham Lincoln	978-89-6370-522-4
who? 10	Martin Luther King, Jr.	978-89-6370-523-1
who? 11	Louis Braille	978-89-6370-439-5
who? 12	Albert Einstein	978-89-6370-440-1
who? 13	Jane Goodall	978-89-6370-441-8
who? 14	Walt Disney	978-89-6370-442-5
who? 15	Winston Churchill	978-89-6370-443-2
who? 16	Warren Buffett	978-89-6370-444-9
who? 17	Nelson Mandela	978-89-6370-445-6
who? 18	Steve Jobs	978-89-6370-446-3
who? 19	J. K. Rowling	978-89-6370-447-0
who? 20	Jean-Henri Fabre	978-89-6370-448-7
who? 21	Vincent van Gogh	978-89-6370-449-4
who? 22	Marie Curie	978-89-6370-450-0
who? 23	Henry David Thoreau	978-89-6370-451-7
who? 24	Andrew Carnegie	978-89-6370-452-4
who? 25	Coco Chanel	978-89-6370-453-1
who? 26	Charlie Chaplin	978-89-6370-454-8
who? 27	Ho Chi Minh	978-89-6370-455-5
who? 28	Ludwig van Beethoven	978-89-6370-456-2
who? 29	Mao Zedong	978-89-6370-457-9
who? 30	Kim Dae-jung	978-89-6370-458-6